To:_____

From:_____

# A Little Book of

# h⬤pe

Freeman-Smith, LLC.
Nashville, TN 37202

*The quoted ideas expressed in this book (but not Scripture verses) are not, in all cases, exact quotations, as some have been edited for clarity and brevity. In all cases, the author has attempted to maintain the speaker's original intent. In some cases, quoted material for this book was obtained from secondary sources, primarily print media. While every effort was made to ensure the accuracy of these sources, the accuracy cannot be guaranteed. For additions, deletions, corrections, or clarifications in future editions of this text, please write Freeman-Smith, LLC.*

The Holy Bible, King James Version

The Holy Bible, New King James Version (NKJV) Copyright © 1982 by Thomas Nelson, Inc. Used by permission.

The Holman Christian Standard Bible™ (HCSB) Copyright © 1999, 2000, 2001 by Holman Bible Publishers. Used by permission.

The New American Standard Bible®, (NASB) Copyright © 1960, 1962, 1963, 1968, 1971, 1972, 1973, 1975, 1977, 1995 by The Lockman Foundation. Used by permission.

Cover Design by Kim Russell / Wahoo Designs
Page Layout by Bart Dawson

ISBN 978-1-60587-230-8

Printed in the United States of America

# A Little Book of

# hope

# Table of Contents

Now may the God of hope fill you
with all joy and peace
in believing, so that you may
overflow with hope
by the power of the Holy Spirit.

—

Romans 15:13 HCSB

# Introduction

Today and every day, the sun rises upon a world filled with God's presence and His love. As believing Christians, we have so many reasons to be hopeful: The Father is in His heaven, His love is everlasting, and we, His children, are blessed beyond measure. Yet sometimes we find ourselves distracted by the demands, the frustrations, and the uncertainties of daily life. But even during our darkest days, God never leaves us for an instant. And even when our hopes are dimmed, God's light still shines brightly. As followers of God's Son, we are called to search for that light—and to keep searching for it as long as we live.

This text celebrates the hope that springs from the promises contained in God's Holy Word. These pages contain inspirational Bible verses, thought-provoking quotations, and

brief essays—all of which can lift your spirits and guide your path.

So today, as you embark upon the next step of your life's journey, think of ways that you can find—and share—the promises that God has made to those who choose to follow in the footsteps of His Son. When you do, you'll discover that hope is like honey: It's hard to spread it around without getting some on yourself.

# Chapter 1

# Hope for the Future

*For I know the thoughts that I think toward you, says the Lord,*
*thoughts of peace and not of evil, to give you a future and a hope.*
*Then you will call upon Me and go and pray to Me,*
*and I will listen to you.*

—

Jeremiah 29:11-12 NKJV

How bright is your future? The answer, in all likelihood, is that your future is so bright that you'd better wear shades!

Now, here's something else to ponder: How bright do you believe your future to be? Are you expecting a terrific tomorrow, or are you dreading a terrible one? And make no mistake: the answers to this second set of questions will have a powerful impact on the way tomorrow turns out.

Corrie ten Boom had this advice: "Never be afraid to trust an unknown future to a known God." And it's advice that most certainly applies to you. So, with no further ado, it's time to trust God . . . and put on the shades.

# Hope for the Future

You can look forward with hope, because one day there will be no more separation, no more scars, and no more suffering in My Father's House. It's the home of your dreams!

Anne Graham Lotz

The future lies all before us. Shall it only be a slight advance upon what we usually do? Ought it not to be a bound, a leap forward to altitudes of endeavor and success undreamed of before?

Annie Armstrong

Every saint has a past—every sinner has a future!

Anonymous

Allow your dreams a place in your prayers and plans. God-given dreams can help you move into the future He is preparing for you.

Barbara Johnson

16     The Christian believes in a fabulous future.

Billy Graham

Every experience God gives us, every person he brings into our lives, is the perfect preparation for the future that only he can see.

Corrie ten Boom

Take courage. We walk in the wilderness today and in the Promised Land tomorrow.

D. L. Moody

Don't ever forget there are more firsts to come.

Dennis Swanberg

17

Our future may look fearfully intimidating, yet we can look up to the Engineer of the Universe, confident that nothing escapes His attention or slips out of the control of those strong hands.

Elisabeth Elliot

*Do not boast about tomorrow, for you do not know what a day may bring forth.*

Proverbs 27:1 NKJV

*For now we see indistinctly, as in a mirror, but then face to face. Now I know in part, but then I will know fully, as I am fully known.*

1 Corinthians 13:12 HCSB

*However, each one must live his life in the situation the Lord assigned when God called him.*

1 Corinthians 7:17 HCSB

## Hope for the Future

*The earth and everything in it, the world and its inhabitants, belong to the Lord.*

Psalm 24:1 HCSB

*My cup runs over. Surely goodness and mercy shall follow me all the days of my life; and I will dwell in the house of the Lord forever.*

Psalm 23:5-6 NKJV

*For God has not given us a spirit of fearfulness, but one of power, love, and sound judgment.*

2 Timothy 1:7 HCSB

20

Joy comes from knowing God loves me
and knows who I am and where
I'm going . . . that my future is secure
as I rest in Him.

—

James Dobson

# Chapter 2

# Experiencing God's Love

*The one who has My commandments and keeps them is the one*
*who loves Me. And the one who loves Me will be loved by*
*My Father. I also will love him and will reveal Myself to him.*

—

John 14:21 HCSB

God loves you—His love for you is deeper and more profound than you can imagine. God's love for you is so great that He sent His only Son to this earth to die for your sins and to offer you the priceless gift of eternal life.

You must decide whether or not to accept God's gift. Will you ignore it or embrace it? Will you return it or neglect it? Will you invite Christ to dwell in the center of your heart, or will you relegate Him to a position of lesser importance? The decision is yours, and so are the consequences. So choose wisely . . . and choose today.

22

Though we may not act like our Father, there is no greater truth than this: We are his. Unalterably. He loves us. Undyingly. Nothing can separate us from the love of Christ.

Max Lucado

The springs of love are in God, not in us.

Oswald Chambers

23

"How can I give you up, Ephraim? How can I hand you over, Israel?" Substitute your own name for Ephraim and Israel. At the heart of the gospel is a God who deliberately surrenders to the wild, irresistible power of love.

Philip Yancey

Incomprehensible and immutable is the love of God. For it was not after we were reconciled to him by the blood of his Son that he began to love us, but he loved us before the foundation of the world, that with his only begotten Son we too might be sons of God before we were any thing at all.

St. Augustine

24

Jesus loves us with fidelity, purity, constancy, and passion, no matter how imperfect we are.

Stormie Omartian

Snuggle in God's arms. When you are hurting, when you feel lonely or left out, let Him cradle you, comfort you, reassure you of His all-sufficient power and love.

Kay Arthur

God loves us the way we are, but He loves us too much to leave us that way.

Leighton Ford

Believing that you are loved will set you free to be who God created you to be. So rest in His love and just be yourself.

Lisa Whelchel

25

The fact is, God no longer deals with us in judgment but in mercy. If people got what they deserved, this old planet would have ripped apart at the seams centuries ago. Praise God that because of His great love "we are not consumed, for his compassions never fail" (Lam. 3:22).

Joni Eareckson Tada

*We love Him because He first loved us.*

1 John 4:19 NKJV

26

*Draw near to God, and He will draw near to you.*

James 4:8 HCSB

*For He is gracious and compassionate, slow to anger, rich in faithful love.*

Joel 2:13 HCSB

*For God loved the world in this way: He gave His only Son, so that everyone who believes in Him will not perish but have eternal life.*

John 3:16 HCSB

*For the Lord is good, and His love is eternal; His faithfulness endures through all generations.*

27

Psalm 100:5 HCSB

*Love consists in this: not that we loved God, but that He loved us and sent His Son to be the propitiation for our sins.*

1 John 4:10 HCSB

28

God has pursued us from farther
than space and longer than time.

—

John Eldredge

# Chapter 3

# Trust Him

*Let us hold fast the confession of our hope without wavering,
for He who promised is faithful.*

—

Hebrews 10:23 NKJV

Are you tired? Discouraged? Fearful? Be comforted and trust God. Are you worried or anxious? Be confident in God's power. He will never desert you. Do you see no hope for the future? Be courageous and call upon God. He will protect you and then use you according to His purposes. Are you grieving? Know that God hears your suffering. He will comfort you and, in time, He will dry your tears. Are you confused? Listen to the quiet voice of your Heavenly Father. He is not a God of confusion. Talk with Him; listen to Him; trust Him. He is steadfast, and He is your Protector . . . forever.

## Trust Him

Do not be afraid, then, that if you trust, or tell others to trust, the matter will end there. Trust is only the beginning and the continual foundation. When we trust Him, the Lord works, and His work is the important part of the whole matter.

Hannah Whitall Smith

Brother, is your faith looking upward today? / Trust in the promise of the Savior. / Sister, is the light shining bright on your way? / Trust in the promise of thy Lord.

Fanny Crosby

God is God. He knows what he is doing. When you can't trace his hand, trust his heart.

Max Lucado

Beware of trusting in yourself, and see that you trust in the Lord.

Oswald Chambers

Sometimes the very essence of faith is trusting God in the midst of things He knows good and well we cannot comprehend.

Beth Moore

Are you serious about wanting God's guidance to become the person he wants you to be? The first step is to tell God that you know you can't manage your own life; that you need his help.

Catherine Marshall

## Trust Him

Never be afraid to trust an unknown future to a known God.

Corrie ten Boom

The hope we have in Jesus is the anchor for the soul—something sure and steadfast, preventing drifting or giving way, lowered to the depth of God's love.

Franklin Graham

As God's children, we are the recipients of lavish love—a love that motivates us to keep trusting even when we have no idea what God is doing.

Beth Moore

*Those who know Your name trust in You because You have not abandoned those who seek You, Lord.*

Psalm 9:10 HCSB

34

*For the Lord God is a sun and shield. The Lord gives grace and glory; He does not withhold the good from those who live with integrity. Lord of Hosts, happy is the person who trusts in You!*

Psalm 84:11-12 HCSB

*O Lord my God, in You I put my trust; save me from all those who persecute me; and deliver me . . . .*

Psalm 7:1 NKJV

## Trust Him

*Trust in Him at all times, you people; pour out your heart before Him; God is a refuge for us.*

Psalm 62:8 NKJV

*The fear of man is a snare, but the one who trusts in the Lord is protected.*

Proverbs 29:25 HCSB

*The one who understands a matter finds success, and the one who trusts in the Lord will be happy.*

Proverbs 16:20 HCSB

For we walk by faith, not by sight.

—

2 Corinthians 5:7 NKJV

36

# Chapter 4

# Overcoming Tough Times

*We are pressured in every way but not crushed;*
*we are perplexed but not in despair.*

—

2 Corinthians 4:8 HCSB

All of us face those occasional days when the traffic jams and the dog gobbles up the homework. But, when we find ourselves overtaken by the minor frustrations of life, we must catch ourselves, take a deep breath, and lift our thoughts upward.

38

Although we must occasionally struggle to rise above the distractions and disappointments of everyday living, we need never struggle alone. God is here—eternally and faithfully, with infinite patience and love. And our friends and family members can help us restore perspective and peace to our souls.

# Overcoming Tough Times

Any man can sing in the day. It is easy to sing when we can read the notes by daylight, but he is the skillful singer who can sing when there is not a ray of light by which to read. Songs in the night come only from God; they are not in the power of man.

C. H. Spurgeon

Speak the name of "Jesus," and all your storms will fold their thunderbolts and leave.

Calvin Miller

Oftentimes, God demonstrates His faithfulness in adversity by providing for us what we need to survive. He does not change our painful circumstances. He sustains us through them.

Charles Swindoll

If your every human plan and calculation has miscarried, if, one by one, human props have been knocked out...take heart. God is trying to get a message through to you, and the message is: "Stop depending on inadequate human resources. Let me handle the matter."

Catherine Marshall

40

Adversity is not simply a tool. It is God's most effective tool for the advancement of our spiritual lives. The circumstances and events that we see as setbacks are oftentimes the very things that launch us into periods of intense spiritual growth. Once we begin to understand this, and accept it as a spiritual fact of life, adversity becomes easier to bear.

Charles Stanley

## Overcoming Tough Times

The kingdom of God is a kingdom of paradox where, through the ugly defeat of a cross, a holy God is utterly glorified. Victory comes through defeat; healing through brokenness; finding self through losing self.

Chuck Colson

In order to realize the worth of the anchor, we need to feel the stress of the storm.

Corrie ten Boom

The hope we have in Jesus is the anchor for the soul—something sure and steadfast, preventing drifting or giving way, lowered to the depth of God's love.

Franklin Graham

*I called to the Lord in my distress; I called to my God. From His temple He heard my voice.*

2 Samuel 22:7 HCSB

*I will be with you when you pass through the waters . . . when you walk through the fire . . . the flame will not burn you. For I the Lord your God, the Holy One of Israel, and your Savior.*

42

Isaiah 43:2-3 HCSB

*When you are in distress and all these things have happened to you, you will return to the Lord your God in later days and obey Him. He will not leave you, destroy you, or forget the covenant with your fathers that He swore to them by oath, because the Lord your God is a compassionate God.*

Deuteronomy 4:30-31 HCSB

## Overcoming Tough Times

*Consider it a great joy, my brothers, whenever you experience various trials, knowing that the testing of your faith produces endurance. But endurance must do its complete work, so that you may be mature and complete, lacking nothing.*

James 1:2-4 HCSB

*We also rejoice in our afflictions, because we know that affliction produces endurance, endurance produces proven character, and proven character produces hope.*

Romans 5:3-4 HCSB

*Dear friends, when the fiery ordeal arises among you to test you, don't be surprised by it, as if something unusual were happening to you. Instead, as you share in the sufferings of the Messiah rejoice, so that you may also rejoice with great joy at the revelation of His glory.*

1 Peter 4:12-13 HCSB

Oh, remember this: There is never a time
when we may not hope in God.
Whatever our necessities, however great our
difficulties, and though to all appearance,
help is impossible, yet our business is to
hope in God, and it will be found
that it is not in vain.

—

George Mueller

# Chapter 5

# Expecting
# God's Abundance

*I have come that they may have life,*
*and that they may have it more abundantly.*

—

John 10:10 NKJV

46

The 10th chapter of John tells us that Christ came to earth so that our lives might be filled with abundance. But what, exactly, did Jesus mean when He promised "life...more abundantly"? Was He referring to material possessions or financial wealth? Hardly. Jesus offers a different kind of abundance: a spiritual richness that extends beyond the temporal boundaries of this world. This everlasting abundance is available to all who seek it and claim it. May we, as believers, claim the riches of Christ Jesus every day that we live, and may we share His blessings with all who cross our path.

God is the giver, and we are the receivers. And His richest gifts are bestowed not upon those who do the greatest things, but upon those who accept His abundance and His grace.

Hannah Whitall Smith

If we just give God the little that we have, we can trust Him to make it go around.

Gloria Gaither

People, places, and things were never meant to give us life. God alone is the author of a fulfilling life.

Gary Smalley & John Trent

If we were given all we wanted here, our hearts would settle for this world rather than the next.

Elisabeth Elliot

48

The only way you can experience abundant life is to surrender your plans to Him.

Charles Stanley

It would be wrong to have a "poverty complex," for to think ourselves paupers is to deny either the King's riches or to deny our being His children.

Catherine Marshall

Instead of living a black-and-white existence, we'll be released into a Technicolor world of vibrancy and emotion when we more accurately reflect His nature to the world around us.

Bill Hybels

God's riches are beyond anything we could ask or even dare to imagine! If my life gets gooey and stale, I have no excuse.

49

Barbara Johnson

If you want purpose and meaning and satisfaction and fulfillment and peace and hope and joy and abundant life that lasts forever, look to Jesus.

Anne Graham Lotz

*And God is able to make every grace overflow to you, so that in every way, always having everything you need, you may excel in every good work.*

2 Corinthians 9:8 HCSB

50

*Until now you have asked for nothing in My name. Ask and you will receive, that your joy may be complete.*

John 16:24 HCSB

*I am the Alpha and the Omega, the Beginning and the End. I will give to the thirsty from the spring of living water as a gift.*

Revelation 21:6 HCSB

## Expecting God's Abundance

*And He said to them, "Take heed and beware of covetousness, for one's life does not consist in the abundance of the things he possesses."*

Luke 12:15 NKJV

*These things have I spoken unto you, that my joy might remain in you, and that your joy might be full.*

51

John 15:11 KJV

*Remember this: the person who sows sparingly will also reap sparingly, and the person who sows generously will also reap generously.*

2 Corinthians 9:6 HCSB

Jesus wants Life for us,
Life with a capital L.

52

—

John Eldredge

# Chapter 6

# Your Daily Devotional

*He awakens [Me] each morning; He awakens My ear to listen like those being instructed. The Lord God has opened My ear, and I was not rebellious; I did not turn back.*

—

Isaiah 50:4-5 HCSB

E ach new day is a gift from God, and if we are wise, we spend a few quiet moments each morning thanking the Giver. Daily life is woven together with the threads of habit, and no habit is more important to our spiritual health than the discipline of daily prayer and devotion to the Creator.

54

When we begin each day with heads bowed and hearts lifted, we remind ourselves of God's love, His protection, and His commandments. And if we are wise, we align our priorities for the coming day with the teachings and commandments that God has given us through His Holy Word.

Are you seeking to change some aspect of your life? Do you seek to improve the condition of your spiritual or physical health? If so, ask for God's help and ask for it many times each day . . . starting with your morning devotional.

How motivating it has been for me to view my early morning devotions as time of retreat alone with Jesus, Who desires that I "come with Him by myself to a quiet place" in order to pray, read His Word, listen for His voice, and be renewed in my spirit.

Anne Graham Lotz

55

Think of this—we may live together with Him here and now, a daily walking with Him who loved us and gave Himself for us.

Elisabeth Elliot

Our devotion to God is strengthened when we offer Him a fresh commitment each day.

Elizabeth George

I believe the reason so many are failing today is that they have not disciplined themselves to read God's Word consistently, day in and day out, and to apply it to every situation in life.

Kay Arthur

There is no way to draw closer to God unless you are in the Word of God every day. It's your compass. Your guide. You can't get where you need to go without it.

Stormie Omartian

56

Knowing God involves an intimate, personal relationship that is developed over time through prayer and getting answers to prayer, through Bible study and applying its teaching to our lives, through obedience and experiencing the power of God, through moment-by-moment submission to Him that results in a moment-by-moment filling of the Holy Spirit.

Anne Graham Lotz

God is a place of safety you can run to, but it helps if you are running to Him on a daily basis so that you are in familiar territory.

Stormie Omartian

We must appropriate the tender mercy of God every day after conversion or problems quickly develop. We need his grace daily in order to live a righteous life.

Jim Cymbala

I don't buy the cliché that quality time is the most important thing. If you don't have enough quantity, you won't get quality.

Leighton Ford

*Be silent before the Lord and wait expectantly for Him.*

Psalm 37:7 HCSB

58

*In quietness and confidence shall be your strength.*

Isaiah 30:15 NKJV

*Be still, and know that I am God.*

Psalm 46:10 NKJV

*Don't worry about anything, but in everything, through prayer and petition with thanksgiving, let your requests be made known to God.*

Philippians 4:6 HCSB

*Your Father knows the things you have need of before you ask Him.*

59

Matthew 6:8 NKJV

*So He Himself often withdrew into the wilderness and prayed.*

Luke 5:16 NKJV

60

Then He spoke a parable to them,
that men always ought to pray
and not lose heart.

—

Luke 18:1 NKJV

# Chapter 7

# The Peace That Passes All Understanding

*And the peace of God, which surpasses every thought, will guard your hearts and your minds in Christ Jesus. Finally brothers, whatever is true, whatever is honorable, whatever is just, whatever is pure, whatever is lovely, whatever is commendable—if there is any moral excellence and if there is any praise—dwell on these things.*

—

Philippians 4:7-8 HCSB

Have you found the genuine peace that can be yours through Jesus Christ? Or are you still rushing after the illusion of "peace and happiness" that the world promises but cannot deliver? The beautiful words of John 14:27 remind us that Jesus offers us peace, not as the world gives, but as He alone gives. Our challenge is to accept Christ's peace into our hearts and then, as best we can, to share His peace with our neighbors.

Today, as a gift to yourself, to your family, and to your friends, claim the inner peace that is your spiritual birthright: the peace of Jesus Christ. It is offered freely; it has been paid for in full; it is yours for the asking. So ask. And then share.

## The Peace That Passes All Understanding

God's peace is like a river, not a pond. In other words, a sense of health and well-being, both of which are expressions of the Hebrew shalom, can permeate our homes even when we're in white-water rapids.

Beth Moore

When you and I are related to Jesus Christ, our strength and wisdom and peace and joy and love and hope may run out, but His life rushes in to keep us filled to the brim. We are showered with blessings, not because of anything we have or have not done, but simply because of Him.

Anne Graham Lotz

Peace is the deepest thing a human personality can know; it is almighty.

Oswald Chambers

We're prone to want God to change our circumstances, but He wants to change our character. We think that peace comes from the outside in, but it comes from the inside out.

Warren Wiersbe

64

Thou hast formed us for Thyself, and our hearts are restless till they find rest in Thee.

St. Augustine

What peace can they have who are not at peace with God?

Matthew Henry

# The Peace That Passes All Understanding

God has promised us abundance, peace, and eternal life. These treasures are ours for the asking; all we must do is claim them. One of the great mysteries of life is why on earth do so many of us wait so very long to claim them?

Marie T. Freeman

God is in control of history; it's His story. Doesn't that give you a great peace—especially when world events seems so tumultuous and insane?

Kay Arthur

That peace, which has been described and which believers enjoy, is a participation of the peace which their glorious Lord and Master himself enjoys.

Jonathan Edwards

*If possible, on your part, live at peace with everyone.*

Romans 12:18 HCSB

66

*Abundant peace belongs to those who love Your instruction; nothing makes them stumble.*

Psalm 119:165 HCSB

*Blessed are the peacemakers, for they shall be called sons of God.*

Matthew 5:9 NKJV

*And suddenly there was with the angel a multitude of the heavenly host praising God and saying: "Glory to God in the highest, and on earth peace, goodwill toward men!"*

Luke 2:13-14 NKJV

*So then, we must pursue what promotes peace and what builds up one another.*

Romans 14:19 HCSB

*For the mind-set of the flesh is death, but the mind-set of the Spirit is life and peace.*

Romans 8:6 HCSB

68

The fruit of our placing all things
in God's hands is the presence
of His abiding peace in our hearts.

—

Hannah Whitall Smith

# Chapter 8

# Don't Give Up

*But as for you, be strong; don't be discouraged,*
*for your work has a reward.*

—

2 Chronicles 15:7 HCSB

The occasional disappointments and failures of life are inevitable. Such setbacks are simply the price that we must pay for our willingness to take risks as we follow our dreams. But even when we encounter setbacks, we must never lose faith.

The reassuring words of Hebrews 10:36 serve as a comforting reminder that perseverance indeed pays: "You have need of endurance, so that when you have done the will of God, you may receive what was promised" (NASB).

Are you willing to trust God's Word? And are you willing to keep "fighting the good fight," even when you've experienced unexpected difficulties? If so, you may soon be surprised at the creative ways that God finds to help determined people like you . . . people who possess the wisdom and the courage to persevere.

## Don't Give Up

Battles are won in the trenches, in the grit and grime of courageous determination; they are won day by day in the arena of life.

Charles Swindoll

You cannot persevere unless there is a trial in your life. There can be no victories without battles; there can be no peaks without valleys. If you want the blessing, you must be prepared to carry the burden and fight the battle. God has to balance privileges with responsibilities, blessings with burdens, or else you and I will become spoiled, pampered children.

Warren Wiersbe

By perseverance the snail reached the ark.

C. H. Spurgeon

Perseverance is more than endurance. It is endurance combined with absolute assurance and certainty that what we are looking for is going to happen.

Oswald Chambers

Are you a Christian? If you are, how can you be hopeless? Are you so depressed by the greatness of your problems that you have given up all hope? Instead of giving up, would you patiently endure? Would you focus on Christ until you are so preoccupied with him alone that you fall prostrate before him?

Anne Graham Lotz

We are all on our way somewhere. We'll get there if we just keep going.

Barbara Johnson

# Don't Give Up

Only the man who follows the command of Jesus single-mindedly and unresistingly lets his yoke rest upon him, finds his burden easy, and under its gentle pressure receives the power to persevere in the right way.

Dietrich Bonhoeffer

Failure is one of life's most powerful teachers. How we handle our failures determines whether we're going to simply "get by" in life or "press on."

Beth Moore

As we find that it is not easy to persevere in this being "alone with God," we begin to realize that it is because we are not "wholly for God." God has a right to demand that He should have us completely for Himself.

Andrew Murray

*Let us lay aside every weight and the sin that so easily ensnares us, and run with endurance the race that lies before us, keeping our eyes on Jesus, the source and perfecter of our faith.*

Hebrews 12:1-2 HCSB

74

*But endurance must do its complete work, so that you may be mature and complete, lacking nothing.*

James 1:4 HCSB

*Blessed is the man who perseveres under trial, because when he has stood the test, he will receive the crown of life that God has promised to those who love him.*

James 1:12 NIV

## Don't Give Up

*Brothers, I do not consider myself to have taken hold of it. But one thing I do: forgetting what is behind and reaching forward to what is ahead, I pursue as my goal the prize promised by God's heavenly call in Christ Jesus.*

Philippians 3:13-14 HCSB

*If you faint in the day of adversity, your strength is small.*

Proverbs 24:10 NKJV

*Indeed we count them blessed who endure.*

James 5:11 NKJV

76

Though a righteous man falls seven times,
he will get up,
but the wicked will stumble into ruin.

—

Proverbs 24:16 HCSB

# Chapter 9

# The Power of Prayer

*Is anyone among you suffering? He should pray.*
*Is anyone cheerful? He should sing praises.*

—

James 5:13 HCSB

ndrew Murray observed, "Some people pray just to pray, and some people pray to know God." Your task, as maturing believer, is to pray, not out of habit or obligation, but out of a sincere desire to know your Heavenly Father. Through constant prayers, you should petition God, you should praise Him, and you should seek to discover His unfolding plans for your life.

78

Today, reach out to the Giver of all blessings. Turn to Him for guidance and for strength. Invite Him into every corner of your day. Ask Him to teach you and to lead you. And remember that no matter your circumstances, God is never far away; He is here . . . always right here. So pray.

## The Power of Prayer

As we join together in prayer, we draw on God's enabling might in a way that multiplies our own efforts many times over.

Shirley Dobson

The center of power is not to be found in summit meetings or in peace conferences. It is not in Peking or Washington or the United Nations, but rather where a child of God prays in the power of the Spirit for God's will to be done in her life, in her home, and in the world around her.

Ruth Bell Graham

When you ask God to do something, don't ask timidly; put your whole heart into it.

Marie T. Freeman

We must leave it to God to answer our prayers in His own wisest way. Sometimes, we are so impatient and think that God does not answer. God always answers! He never fails! Be still. Abide in Him.

Mrs. Charles E. Cowman

God delights in the prayers of His children—prayers that express our love for Him, prayers that share our deepest burdens with Him.

Billy Graham

Are you weak? Weary? Confused? Troubled? Pressured? How is your relationship with God? Is it held in its place of priority? I believe the greater the pressure, the greater your need for time alone with Him.

Kay Arthur

# The Power of Prayer

The Christian on his knees sees more than the philosopher on tiptoe.

D. L. Moody

On our knees we are the most powerful force on earth.

Billy Graham

Prayer guards hearts and minds and causes God to bring peace out of chaos.

Beth Moore

*Therefore I want the men in every place to pray, lifting up holy hands without anger or argument.*

1 Timothy 2:8 HCSB

*Rejoice always, pray without ceasing, in everything give thanks; for this is the will of God in Christ Jesus for you.*

1 Thessalonians 5:16-18 NKJV

*I will thank the Lord with all my heart; I will declare all Your wonderful works. I will rejoice and boast about You; I will sing about Your name, Most High.*

Psalm 9:1-2 HCSB

# The Power of Prayer

*Rejoice in hope; be patient in affliction; be persistent in prayer.*

Romans 12:12 HCSB

*May my prayer reach Your presence; listen to my cry.*

Psalm 88:2 HCSB

*Therefore let everyone who is faithful pray to You . . . .*

Psalm 32:6 HCSB

Let the words of my mouth
and the meditation of my heart
be acceptable in Your sight, O Lord,
my strength and my Redeemer.

—

Psalm 19:14 NKJV

*trust: assured reliance on the charecter, ability Strength, or truth of someone or something. one in which confidence is placed.*

# He Renews Your Strength

# Chapter 10

*But those who trust in the Lord will renew their strength;*
*they will soar on wings like eagles; they will run*
*and not grow weary; they will walk and not faint.*

—

Isaiah 40:31 HCSB

God's Word is clear: When we genuinely lift our hearts and prayers to Him, He renews our strength. Are you almost too weary to lift your head? Then bow it. Offer your concerns and your fears to your Father in Heaven. He is always at your side, offering His love and His strength.

Are you troubled or anxious? Take your anxieties to God in prayer. Are you weak or worried? Delve deeply into God's Holy Word and sense His presence in the quiet moments of the early morning. Are you spiritually exhausted? Call upon fellow believers to support you, and call upon Christ to renew your spirit and your life. Your Savior will not let you down. To the contrary, He will lift you up when you ask Him to do so. So what, dear friend, are you waiting for?

He is the God of wholeness and restoration.

Stormie Omartian

Repentance removes old sins and wrong attitudes, and it opens the way for the Holy Spirit to restore our spiritual health.

Shirley Dobson

For centuries now, Christians have poured out their hearts to the Lord and found treasured moments of refuge.

Bill Hybels

Whoever you are, whatever your condition or circumstance, whatever your past or problem, Jesus can restore you to wholeness.

Anne Graham Lotz

Troubles we bear trustfully can bring us a fresh vision of God and a new outlook on life, an outlook of peace and hope.

Billy Graham

How motivating it has been for me to view my early morning devotions as time of retreat alone with Jesus, Who desires that I "come with Him by myself to a quiet place" in order to pray, read His Word, listen for His voice, and be renewed in my spirit.

Anne Graham Lotz

When we invite Jesus into our lives, we experience life in the fullest, most vital sense.

Catherine Marshall

Jesus is calling the weary to rest, / Calling today, calling today, / Bring Him your burden and you shall be blest; / He will not turn you away.

Fanny Crosby

The same voice that brought Lazarus out of the tomb raised us to newness of life.

C. H. Spurgeon

*Therefore we were buried with Him by baptism into death, in order that, just as Christ was raised from the dead by the glory of the Father, so we too may walk in a new way of life.*

Romans 6:4 HCSB

*And do not be conformed to this world, but be transformed by the renewing of your mind, that you may prove what is that good and acceptable and perfect will of God.*

Romans 12:2 NKJV

*Then the One seated on the throne said, "Look! I am making everything new."*

Revelation 21:5 HCSB

## He Renews Your Strength

*God, create a clean heart for me and renew a steadfast spirit within me.*

Psalm 51:10 HCSB

*He makes me to lie down in green pastures; He leads me beside the still waters. He restores my soul; He leads me in the paths of righteousness for His name's sake.*

Psalm 23:2-3 NKJV

*Take My yoke upon you and learn from Me, because I am gentle and humble in heart, and you will find rest for your souls. For My yoke is easy and My burden is light.*

Matthew 11:29-30 HCSB

92

*"For I will restore health to you*
*and heal you of your wounds,"*
*says the Lord.*

—

Jeremiah 30:17 NKJV

# Chapter 11

# Never Lose Hope

*But if we hope for what we do not see,*
*we eagerly wait for it with patience.*

—

Romans 8:25 HCSB

Despite God's promises, despite Christ's love, and despite our countless blessings, we frail human beings can still lose hope from time to time. When we do, we need the encouragement of Christian friends, the life-changing power of prayer, and the healing truth of God's Holy Word. If we find ourselves falling into the spiritual traps of worry and discouragement, we should seek the healing touch of Jesus and the encouraging words of fellow Christians. Even though this world can be a place of trials and struggles, God has promised us peace, joy, and eternal life if we give ourselves to Him. And, of course, God keeps His promises today, tomorrow, and forever.

## Never Lose Hope

Never yield to gloomy anticipation. Place your hope and confidence in God. He has no record of failure.

Mrs. Charles E. Cowman

No other religion, no other philosophy promises new bodies, hearts, and minds. Only in the Gospel of Christ do hurting people find such incredible hope.

Joni Eareckson Tada

Oh, remember this: There is never a time when we may not hope in God. Whatever our necessities, however great our difficulties, and though to all appearance help is impossible, yet our business is to hope in God, and it will be found that it is not in vain.

George Mueller

I wish I could make it all new again; I can't. But God can. "He restores my soul," wrote the shepherd. God doesn't reform; he restores. He doesn't camouflage the old; he restores the new. The Master Builder will pull out the original plan and restore it. He will restore the vigor, he will restore the energy. He will restore the hope. He will restore the soul.

Max Lucado

96

The best we can hope for in this life is a knothole peek at the shining realities ahead. Yet a glimpse is enough. It's enough to convince our hearts that whatever sufferings and sorrows currently assail us aren't worthy of comparison to that which waits over the horizon.

Joni Eareckson Tada

## Never Lose Hope

Faith looks back and draws courage; hope looks ahead and keeps desire alive.

John Eldredge

I discovered that sorrow was not to be feared but rather endured with hope and expectancy that God would use it to visit and bless my life.

Jill Briscoe

Hope is nothing more than the expectation of those things which faith has believed to be truly promised by God.

John Calvin

Love is the seed of all hope. It is the enticement to trust, to risk, to try, and to go on.

Gloria Gaither

*Now may the God of hope fill you with all joy and peace in believing,*
*so that you may overflow with hope by the power of the Holy Spirit.*
Romans 15:13 HCSB

98

*Rejoice in hope; be patient in affliction; be persistent in prayer.*
Romans 12:12 HCSB

*But I will hope continually and will praise You more and more.*
Psalm 71:14 HCSB

## Never Lose Hope

*We have this hope—like a sure and firm anchor of the soul—that enters the inner sanctuary behind the curtain.*

Hebrews 6:19 HCSB

*Let us hold on to the confession of our hope without wavering, for He who promised is faithful.*

Hebrews 10:23 HCSB

*Therefore we do not lose heart. Even though our outward man is perishing, yet the inward man is being renewed day by day.*

2 Corinthians 4:16 NKJV

100

Hope looks for the good in people,
opens doors for people, discovers
what can be done to help, lights a candle,
does not yield to cynicism.
Hope sets people free.

—

Barbara Johnson

# Chapter 12

# Living on Purpose

*For it is God who is working among you both
the willing and the working for His good purpose.*

—

Philippians 2:13 HCSB

"What does God intend for me to do with the rest of my life?" It's an easy question to ask, but, for many of us, a difficult question to answer. Why? Because God's purposes aren't always clear to us. Sometimes we wander aimlessly in a spiritual desert of our own design. And sometimes, we struggle mightily against God in a vain effort to find success and happiness through the world's means, not His.

How can we know precisely what God's plans are for our lives? The answer, of course, is that we cannot know precisely what God intends; what we can do is this: we can study His Word, we can pray for His guidance, we can obey His commandments; and we can trust His direction. And that is precisely what we should do.

Without God, life has no purpose, and without purpose, life has no meaning.

Rick Warren

Continually restate to yourself what the purpose of your life is.

Oswald Chambers

Blessed are those who know what on earth they are here on earth to do and set themselves about the business of doing it.

Max Lucado

God never calls without enabling us. In other words, if he calls you to do something, he makes it possible for you to do it.

Luci Swindoll

104

Each one of us is God's special work of art. Through us, He teaches and inspires, delights and encourages, informs and uplifts all those who view our lives. God, the master artist, is most concerned about expressing Himself—His thoughts and His intentions—through what He paints in our character.... [He] wants to paint a beautiful portrait of His Son in and through your life. A painting like no other in all of time.

Joni Eareckson Tada

We may run, walk, stumble, drive, or fly, but let us never lose sight of the reason for the journey, or miss a chance to see a rainbow on the way.

Gloria Gaither

God is more concerned with the direction of your life than with its speed.

Marie T. Freeman

How much of our lives are, well, so daily. How often our hours are filled with the mundane, seemingly unimportant things that have to be done, whether at home or work. These very "daily" tasks could become a celebration of praise. "It is through consecration," someone has said, "that drudgery is made divine."

Gigi Graham Tchividjian

*We know that all things work together for the good of those who love God: those who are called according to His purpose.*

Romans 8:28 HCSB

106

*I will instruct you and show you the way to go; with My eye on you, I will give counsel.*

Psalm 32:8 HCSB

*You reveal the path of life to me; in Your presence is abundant joy; in Your right hand are eternal pleasures.*

Psalm 16:11 HCSB

## Living on Purpose

*Commit your activities to the Lord and your plans will be achieved.*

Proverbs 16:3 HCSB

*Whatever you do, do all to the glory of God.*

1 Corinthians 10:31 NKJV

*To everything there is a season, a time for every purpose under heaven.*

Ecclesiastes 3:1 NKJV

108

When we realize and embrace
the Lord's will for us, we will love to do it.
We won't want to do anything else.
It's a passion.

—

Franklin Graham

# Chapter 13

# Finding and Keeping Happiness

*How happy are those whose way is blameless,
who live according to the law of the Lord! Happy are those who
keep His decrees and seek Him with all their heart.*

—

Psalm 119:1-2 HCSB

Happiness depends less upon our circumstances than upon our thoughts. When we turn our thoughts to God, to His gifts, and to His glorious creation, we experience the joy that God intends for His children. But, when we focus on the negative aspects of life, we suffer needlessly.

Do you sincerely want to be a happy Christian? Then set your mind and your heart upon God's love and His grace. The fullness of life in Christ is available to all who seek it and claim it. Count yourself among that number. Seek first the salvation that is available through a personal relationship with Jesus Christ, and then claim the joy, the peace, and the spiritual abundance that the Shepherd offers His sheep.

People who have invested their lives in worthwhile have discovered a measure of happiness.

Warren Wiersbe

I became aware of one very important concept I had missed before: my attitude—not my circumstances—was what was making me unhappy.

Vonette Bright

We will never be happy until we make God the source of our fulfillment and the answer to our longings.

Stormie Omartian

The secret of a happy life is to delight in duty. When duty becomes delight, then burdens become blessings.

Warren Wiersbe

This is the happy life: to rejoice to Thee, of Thee, for Thee; this it is, and there is no other.

St. Augustine

I am truly happy with Jesus Christ. I couldn't live without Him.

Ruth Bell Graham

Christ is the secret, the source, the substance, the center, and the circumference of all true and lasting gladness.

Mrs. Charles E. Cowman

God's goal is not to make you happy. It is to make you his.     113

Max Lucado

Our thoughts, not our circumstances, determine our happiness.

John Maxwell

*Happy is the one whose help is the God of Jacob, whose hope is in the Lord his God.*

Psalm 146:5 HCSB

114

*How happy is everyone who fears the Lord, who walks in His ways!*

Psalm 128:1 HCSB

*Happy is the man who fears the Lord, taking great delight in His commandments.*

Psalm 112:1 HCSB

*Happy is a man who finds wisdom and who acquires understanding.*

Proverbs 3:13 HCSB

*A joyful heart is good medicine, but a broken spirit dries up the bones.*

Proverbs 17:22 HCSB          115

*Happy are the people whose strength is in You, whose hearts are set on pilgrimage.*

Psalm 84:5 HCSB

116

The happiest people in the world
are not those who have no problems,
but the people who have learned to live
with those things that are less than perfect.

—

James Dobson

# Chapter 14

# Beyond Fear

*Be strong and courageous, and do the work.*
*Don't be afraid or discouraged, for the Lord God, my God,*
*is with you. He won't leave you or forsake you.*

—

1 Chronicles 28:20 HCSB

A storm rose quickly on the Sea of Galilee, and the disciples were afraid. Although they had seen Jesus perform many miracles, the disciples feared for their lives, so they turned to their Savior, and He calmed the waters and the wind.

Sometimes, we, like the disciples, feel threatened by the inevitable storms of life. And when we are fearful, we, too, can turn to Christ for courage and for comfort.

118

The next time you're afraid, remember that the One who calmed the wind and the waves is also your personal Savior. And remember that the ultimate battle has already been won at Calvary. We, as believers, can live courageously in the promises of our Lord . . . and we should.

# Beyond Fear

The truth of Christ brings assurance and so removes the former problem of fear and uncertainty.

A. W. Tozer

If a person fears God, he or she has no reason to fear anything else. On the other hand, if a person does not fear God, then fear becomes a way of life.

Beth Moore

Courage is contagious.

Billy Graham

Daniel looked into the face of God and would not fear the face of a lion.

C. H. Spurgeon

Courage is not simply one of the virtues, but the form of every virtue at the testing point, which means, at the point of highest reality. A chastity or honesty or mercy which yields to danger will be chaste or honest or merciful only on conditions. Pilate was merciful till it became risky.

C. S. Lewis

Our Lord is searching for people who will make a difference. Christians dare not dissolve into the background or blend into the neutral scenery of the world.

Charles Swindoll

## Beyond Fear

With each new experience of letting God be in control, we gain courage and reinforcement for daring to do it again and again.

Gloria Gaither

When once we are assured that God is good, then there can be nothing left to fear.

Hannah Whitall Smith

Are you fearful? First, bow your head and pray for God's strength. Then, raise your head knowing that, together, you and God can handle whatever comes your way.

Jim Gallery

*But when Jesus heard it, He answered him, "Don't be afraid. Only believe."*

Luke 8:50 HCSB

122

*For God has not given us a spirit of fearfulness, but one of power, love, and sound judgment.*

2 Timothy 1:7 HCSB

*Be alert, stand firm in the faith, be brave and strong.*

1 Corinthians 16:13 HCSB

*But He said to them, "Why are you fearful, you of little faith?" Then He got up and rebuked the winds and the sea. And there was a great calm.*

Matthew 8:26 HCSB

*Haven't I commanded you: be strong and courageous? Do not be afraid or discouraged, for the Lord your God is with you wherever you go.*

Joshua 1:9 HCSB

*Be strong and courageous, all you who put your hope in the Lord.*

Psalm 31:24 HCSB

124

There comes a time when we simply
have to face the challenges in our lives
and stop backing down.

—

John Eldredge

# Chapter 15

# Encouraging Others

*I want their hearts to be encouraged and joined together in love,*
*so that they may have all the riches of assured understanding,*
*and have the knowledge of God's mystery—Christ.*

—

Colossians 2:2 HCSB

The words that we speak have the power to do great good or great harm. If we speak words of encouragement and hope, we can lift others up. And that's exactly what God commands us to do!

Sometimes, when we feel uplifted and secure, it's easy to speak kind words. Other times, when we are discouraged or tired, we can scarcely summon the energy to uplift ourselves, much less anyone else. God intends that we speak words of kindness, wisdom, and truth, no matter our circumstances, no matter our emotions. When we do, we share a priceless gift with the world, and we give glory to the One who gave His life for us. As believers, we must do no less.

Make it a rule, and pray to God to help you to keep it, never to lie down at night without being able to say: "I have made at least one human being a little wiser, a little happier, or a little better this day."

Charles Kingsley

God grant that we may not hinder those who are battling their way slowly into the light.

Oswald Chambers

I can usually sense that a leading is from the Holy Spirit when it calls me to humble myself, to serve somebody, to encourage somebody, or to give something away. Very rarely will the evil one lead us to do those kind of things.

Bill Hybels

God is still in the process of dispensing gifts, and He uses ordinary individuals like us to develop those gifts in other people.

Howard Hendricks

128 He climbs highest who helps another up.

Zig Ziglar

No journey is complete that does not lead through some dark valleys. We can properly comfort others only with the comfort we ourselves have been given by God.

Vance Havner

God of our life, there are days when the burdens we carry chafe our shoulders and weigh us down; when the road seems dreary and endless, the skies gray and threatening; when our lives have no music in them, and our hearts are lonely, and our souls have lost their courage. Flood the path with light, run our eyes to where the skies are full of promise; tune our hearts to brave music; give us the sense of comradeship with heroes and saints of every age; and so quicken our spirits that we may be able to encourage the souls of all who journey with us on the road of life, to Your honor and glory.

St. Augustine

129

Encouragement starts at home, but it should never end there.

Marie T. Freeman

*Finally, all of you be of one mind, having compassion for one another; love as brothers, be tenderhearted, be courteous.*

1 Peter 3:8 NKJV

130

*Feed the flock of God which is among you....*

1 Peter 5:2 KJV

*Two are better than one because they have a good reward for their efforts. For if either falls, his companion can lift him up; but pity the one who falls without another to lift him up.*

Ecclesiastes 4:9-10 HCSB

## Encouraging Others

*Carry one another's burdens; in this way you will fulfill the law of Christ.*

Galatians 6:2 HCSB

*And let us be concerned about one another in order to promote love and good works.*

Hebrews 10:24 HCSB

*Therefore encourage one another and build each other up as you are already doing.*

1 Thessalonians 5:11 HCSB

132

One of the ways God refills us after failure is
through the blessing of Christian fellowship.
Just experiencing the joy of simple activities
shared with other children of God
can have a healing effect on us.

—

Anne Graham Lotz

# Chapter 16

# The Wisdom to Be Thankful

*Therefore as you have received Christ Jesus the Lord, walk in Him, rooted and built up in Him and established in the faith, just as you were taught, and overflowing with thankfulness.*

—

Colossians 2:6-7 HCSB

As we begin each day, we should pause to consider God's blessings. God's gifts are, of course, too numerous to count, but as believers, we should attempt to count them nonetheless. Our blessings include life, friends, family, talents, opportunities, and possessions, for starters.

The Greek biographer Plutarch observed, "The worship most acceptable to God comes from a thankful and cheerful heart."

And Marianne Williamson correctly observed, "Joy is what happens to us when we allow ourselves to recognize how good things really are."

So today, as a way of saying thanks the Giver of all things Good, praise His gifts, use His gifts, and share His gifts. God certainly deserves your gratitude, and you certainly deserve the experience of being grateful.

God has promised that if we harvest well with the tools of thanksgiving, there will be seeds for planting in the spring.

Gloria Gaither

It is always possible to be thankful for what is given rather than to complain about what is not given. One or the other becomes a habit of life.

Elisabeth Elliot

A friend is one who makes me do my best.

Oswald Chambers

The joy of the Holy Spirit is experienced by giving thanks in all situations.

Bill Bright

Thank God every morning when you get up that you have something to do that day which must be done, whether you like it or not.

Charles Kingsley

Praise and thank God for who He is and for what He has done for you.

Billy Graham

The words "thank" and "think" come from the same root word. If we would think more, we would thank more.

Warren Wiersbe

God often keeps us on the path by guiding us through the counsel of friends and trusted spiritual advisors.

Bill Hybels

Though I know intellectually how vulnerable I am to pride and power, I am the last one to know when I succumb to their seduction. That's why spiritual Lone Rangers are so dangerous—and why we must depend on trusted brothers and sisters who love us enough to tell us the truth.

Chuck Colson

*Thanks be to God for His indescribable gift.*

2 Corinthians 9:15 HCSB

*And let the peace of the Messiah, to which you were also called in one body, control your hearts. Be thankful.*

138

Colossians 3:15 HCSB

*It is good to give thanks to the Lord, and to sing praises to Your name, O Most High.*

Psalm 92:1 NKJV

## The Wisdom to Be Thankful

*Enter into His gates with thanksgiving, and into His courts with praise. Be thankful to Him, and bless His name. For the Lord is good; His mercy is everlasting, and His truth endures to all generations.*

Psalm 100:4-5 NKJV

*And whatever you do, in word or in deed, do everything in the name of the Lord Jesus, giving thanks to God the Father through Him.*

Colossians 3:17 HCSB

*In everything give thanks; for this is the will of God in Christ Jesus for you.*

1 Thessalonians 5:18 NKJV

140

The act of thanksgiving is a demonstration
of the fact that you are going
to trust and believe God.

—

Kay Arthur

# Chapter 17

# Trusting God's Word

*Heaven and earth will pass away,*
*but My words will never pass away.*

—

Matthew 24:35 HCSB

The Psalmist describes God's Word as, "a light to my path." Is the Bible your lamp? If not, you are depriving yourself of a priceless gift from the Creator. Vance Havner observed, "It takes calm, thoughtful, prayerful meditation on the Word to extract its deepest nourishment." And make no mistake: you need that kind of nourishment.

Are you a woman who trusts God's Word without reservation? Hopefully so, because the Bible is unlike any other book—it is a guidebook for life here on earth and for life eternal.

God's Word can be a light to guide your steps. Claim it as your light today, tomorrow, and every day of your life—and then walk confidently in the footsteps of God's only begotten Son.

Anything that comes to us from the God of the Word will deepen our love for the Word of God.

A. W. Tozer

The Bible is God's Word, given to us by God Himself so we can know Him and His will for our lives.

Billy Graham

Nobody ever outgrows Scripture; the book widens and deepens with our years.

C. H. Spurgeon

God's voice isn't all that difficult to hear. He sometimes shouts through our pain, whispers to us while we're relaxing on vacation, occasionally, He sings to us in a song, and warns us through the sixty-six books of His written Word. It's right there, ink on paper. Count on it—that book will never lead you astray.

Charles Swindoll

144

The Scriptures were not given for our information, but for our transformation.

D. L. Moody

Just as you do not analyze the words of someone you love, but accept them as they are said to you, accept the Word of Scripture and ponder it in your heart.

Dietrich Bonhoeffer

The Gospel is not so much a demand as it is an offer, an offer of new life to man by the grace of God.

E. Stanley Jones

God's Word is a light not only to our path but also to our thinking. Place it in your heart today, and you will never walk in darkness.

Joni Eareckson Tada

Walking in faith brings you to the Word of God. There you will be healed, cleansed, fed, nurtured, equipped, and matured.

Kay Arthur

*But the word of the Lord endures forever. And this is the word that was preached as the gospel to you.*

1 Peter 1:25 HCSB

*All Scripture is inspired by God and is profitable for teaching, for rebuking, for correcting, for training in righteousness, so that the man of God may be complete, equipped for every good work.*

2 Timothy 3:16-17 HCSB

*For the word of God is living and effective and sharper than any two-edged sword, penetrating as far as to divide soul, spirit, joints, and marrow; it is a judge of the ideas and thoughts of the heart.*

Hebrews 4:12 HCSB

*The one who is from God listens to God's words. This is why you don't listen, because you are not from God.*

John 8:47 HCSB

*For I am not ashamed of the gospel, because it is God's power for salvation to everyone who believes.*

147

Romans 1:16 HCSB

*Man shall not live by bread alone, but by every word that proceeds from the mouth of God.*

Matthew 4:4 NKJV

148

You should not believe your conscience
and your feelings more than the word
which the Lord who receives
sinners preaches to you.

—

Martin Luther

# Chapter 18

# The Promise of Eternal Life

*For God so loved the world that He gave His only begotten Son,
that whoever believes in Him should not perish
but have everlasting life.*

—

John 3:16 NKJV

Ours is not a distant God. Ours is a God who understands—far better than we ever could—the essence of what it means to be human. How marvelous it is that God became a man and walked among us. Had He not chosen to do so, we might feel removed from a distant Creator.

150

God understands our hopes, our fears, and our temptations. He understands what it means to be angry and what it costs to forgive. He knows the heart, the conscience, and the soul of every person who has ever lived, including you. And God has a plan of salvation that is intended for you. Accept it. Accept God's gift through the person of His Son Christ Jesus, and then rest assured: God walked among us so that you might have eternal life; amazing though it may seem, He did it for you.

The damage done to us on this earth will never find its way into that safe city. We can relax, we can rest, and though some of us can hardly imagine it, we can prepare to feel safe and secure for all of eternity.

Bill Hybels

151

God's salvation comes as gift; it is eternal, and it is a continuum, meaning it starts when I receive the gift in faith and is never-ending.

Franklin Graham

152

Teach us to set our hopes on heaven,
to hold firmly to the promise of eternal life,
so that we can withstand the struggles
and storms of this world.

—

Max Lucado

Your choice to either receive or reject the Lord Jesus Christ will determine where you spend eternity.

Anne Graham Lotz

If you are a believer, your judgment will not determine your eternal destiny. Christ's finished work on Calvary was applied to you the moment you accepted Christ as Savior.

Beth Moore

Let us see the victorious Jesus: the conqueror of the tomb, the one who defied death. And let us be reminded that we, too, will be granted the same victory!

Max Lucado

I can still hardly believe it. I, with shriveled, bent fingers, atrophied muscles, gnarled knees, and no feeling from the shoulders down, will one day have a new body—light, bright and clothed in righteousness—powerful and dazzling.

Joni Eareckson Tada

154

God has promised us abundance, peace, and eternal life. These treasures are ours for the asking; all we must do is claim them. One of the great mysteries of life is why on earth do so many of us wait so very long to lay claim to God's gifts?

Marie T. Freeman

And because we know Christ is alive,
we have hope for the present
and hope for life beyond the grave.

—

Billy Graham

155

*And this is the testimony: God has given us eternal life, and this life is in His Son. The one who has the Son has life. The one who doesn't have the Son of God does not have life.*

1 John 5:11-12 HCSB

156

*Pursue righteousness, godliness, faith, love, endurance, and gentleness. Fight the good fight for the faith; take hold of eternal life, to which you were called and have made a good confession before many witnesses.*

1 Timothy 6:11-12 HCSB

*Jesus said to her, "I am the resurrection and the life. The one who believes in Me, even if he dies, will live. Everyone who lives and believes in Me will never die—ever. Do you believe this?"*

John 11:25-26 HCSB

*I have written these things to you who believe in the name of the Son of God, so that you may know that you have eternal life.*

1 John 5:13 HCSB

*For if you live according to the flesh you will die; but if by the Spirit you put to death the deeds of the body, you will live.*

157

Romans 8:13 NKJV

*We do not want you to be uninformed, brothers, concerning those who are asleep, so that you will not grieve like the rest, who have no hope. Since we believe that Jesus died and rose again, in the same way God will bring with Him those who have fallen asleep through Jesus.*

1 Thessalonians 4:13-14 HCSB

158

God loves you and wants you
to experience peace and life—
abundant and eternal.

—

Billy Graham

*Now may the God of hope fill you*
*with all joy and peace*
*in believing, so that you may*
*overflow with hope*
*by the power of the Holy Spirit.*

—

Romans 15:13 HCSB

159